SPACE TECH

SPACE SHUTTLES

by ALLAN MOREY

BELLWETHER MEDIA • MINNEAPOLIS, MN

EPIC BOOKS are no ordinary books. They burst with intense action, high-speed heroics, and shadows of the unknown. Are you ready for an Epic adventure?

This edition first published in 2018 by Bellwether Media, Inc.

No part of this publication may be reproduced in whole or in part without written permission of the publisher. For information regarding permission, write to Bellwether Media, Inc., Attention: Permissions Department, 5357 Penn Avenue South, Minneapolis, MN 55419.

Library of Congress Cataloging-in-Publication Data

Names: Morey, Allan.
Title: Space Shuttles / by Allan Morey.
Description: Minneapolis, MN : Bellwether Media, Inc., 2018. | Series: Epic.
   Space Tech | Audience: Age 7-12. | Includes bibliographical references and index.
Identifiers: LCCN 2016052938 (print) | LCCN 2016053147 (ebook) | ISBN 9781626177062 (hardcover : alk. paper) |
   ISBN 9781681034362 (ebook) | ISBN 9781618912893 (paperback : alk. paper)
Subjects: LCSH: Space shuttles–Juvenile literature.
Classification: LCC TL795.515 .M67 2018 (print) | LCC TL795.515 (ebook) | DDC 629.44/1-dc23
LC record available at https://lccn.loc.gov/2016052938

Editor: Nathan Sommer   Designer: Steve Porter

Printed in the United States of America, North Mankato, MN.

TABLE OF CONTENTS

SPACE SHUTTLE AT WORK!

It is July 8, 2011. **NASA** space shuttle *Atlantis* sits on the **launch pad**. Its **rocket boosters** fire. The ground shakes. A rumble fills the air. Liftoff! *Atlantis* sets off on the final space shuttle **mission** ever.

space shuttle
Atlantis

LIFTOFF!

All space shuttle flights
took off at the Kennedy
Space Center in Cape
Canaveral, Florida.

WHAT WAS A SPACE SHUTTLE?

Early **spacecraft** could be used just once. Most crashed into the ocean after a flight. But space shuttles were **reusable**. They had wings like airplanes. They could also land safely on runways.

early spacecraft landing

space shuttle *Atlantis* landing

Space shuttles let humans explore space like never before. The reusable shuttles allowed NASA to fly more missions. They could also stay in **orbit** longer than other spacecraft. This gave **astronauts** more time to do their jobs.

ALL IN A NAME!

NASA space shuttles were named after famous ships.

PARTS OF A SPACE SHUTTLE

Space shuttles had three main parts. Rocket boosters were on the sides. The boosters gave extra power needed for liftoff. They fell off after a few minutes.

rocket
boosters

external
fuel tank

The **external** fuel tank attached to the bottom of the shuttle. It held the fuel needed to power the shuttle into space. The tank fell off once the shuttle was in orbit.

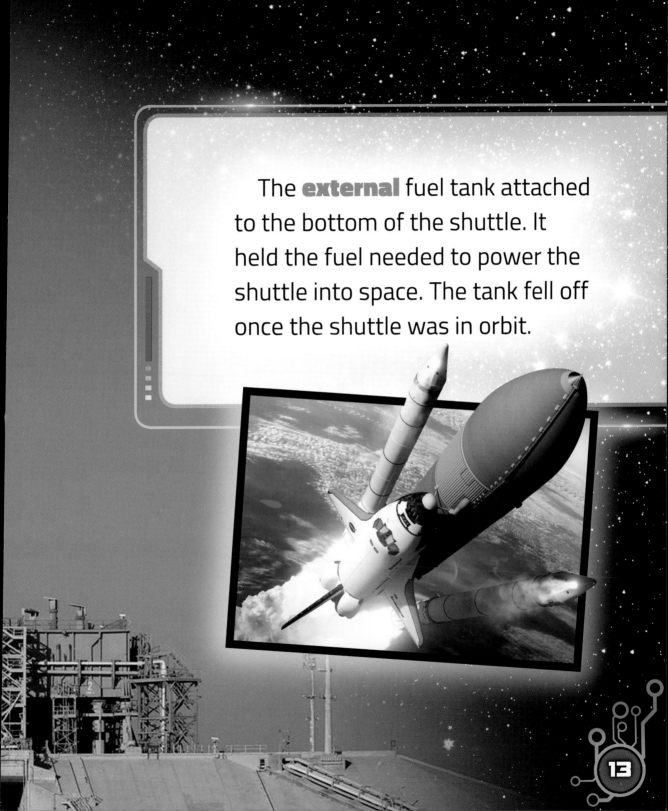

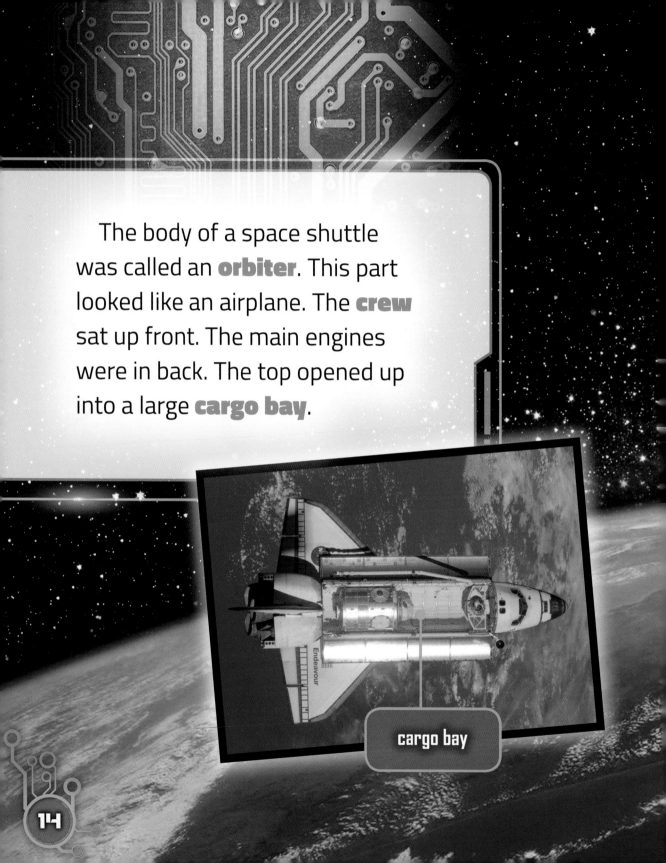

The body of a space shuttle was called an **orbiter**. This part looked like an airplane. The **crew** sat up front. The main engines were in back. The top opened up into a large **cargo bay**.

cargo bay

IDENTIFY THE MACHINE
space shuttle *Endeavour*

rocket
boosters

external
fuel tank

orbiter

cargo bay

main
engines

Endeavour

SPACE SHUTTLE MISSIONS

Space shuttles completed many different missions. Astronauts studied space on shuttles. They launched and repaired **satellites** from them. Shuttles also carried parts to space to help build the **International Space Station** (ISS).

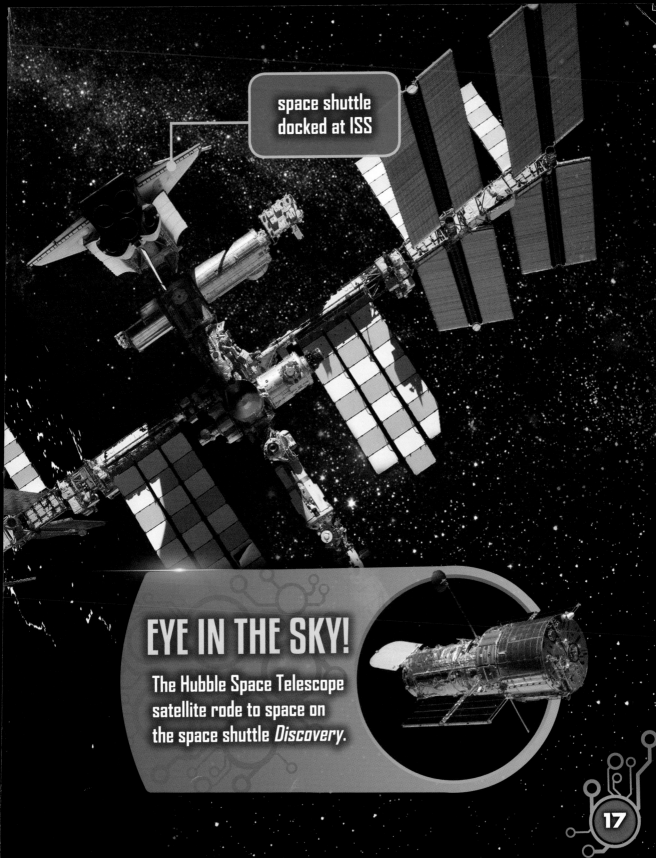

space shuttle
docked at ISS

EYE IN THE SKY!

The Hubble Space Telescope
satellite rode to space on
the space shuttle *Discovery*.

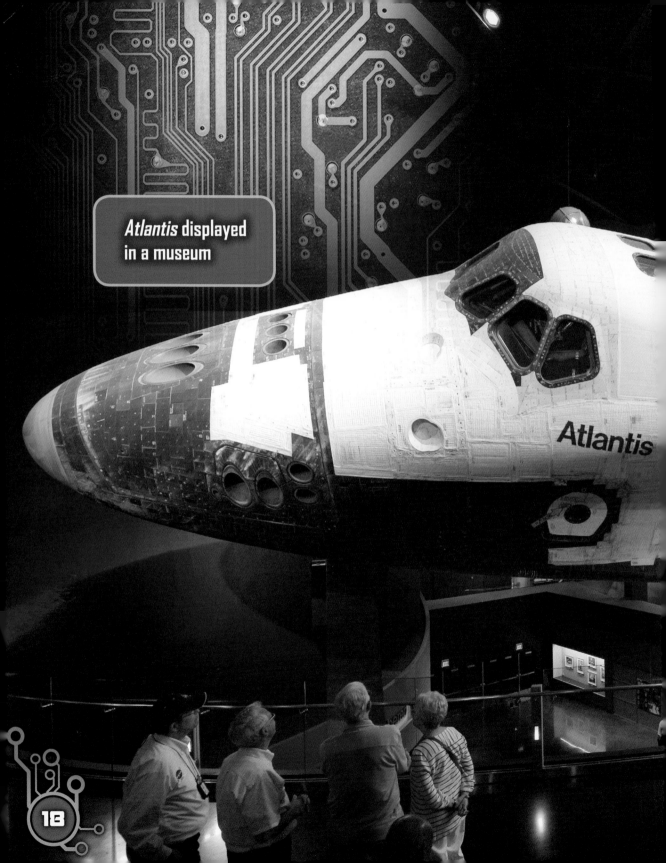

Atlantis displayed in a museum

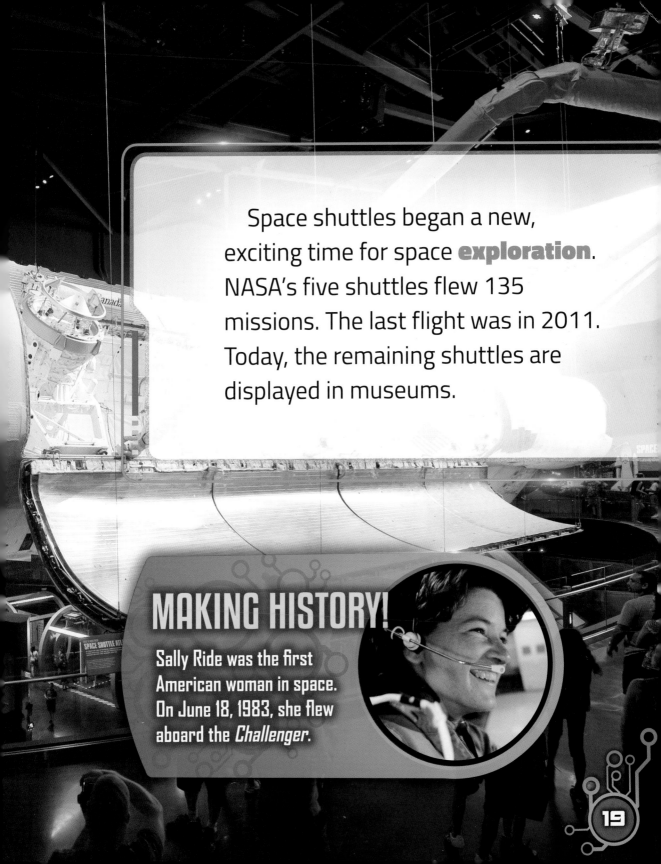

Space shuttles began a new, exciting time for space **exploration**. NASA's five shuttles flew 135 missions. The last flight was in 2011. Today, the remaining shuttles are displayed in museums.

MAKING HISTORY!

Sally Ride was the first American woman in space. On June 18, 1983, she flew aboard the *Challenger*.

DISCOVERY SHUTTLE SPECS

NAME: *DISCOVERY*

missions: carry astronauts and cargo into Earth's orbit and to and from the International Space Station; launch large satellites; serve as an orbiting science laboratory.

first time in space: August 30, 1984

height: 57 feet (17 meters)

location in space: orbits around 190 to 330 miles (306 to 531 kilometers) above Earth

speed: 17,500 mph (28,000 kph)

length: 184 feet (56 meters)

wingspan: 78 feet (24 meters)

GLOSSARY

astronauts—people trained to travel and work in outer space

cargo bay—the area in a vehicle where supplies or other goods are kept

crew—people who work together on a space shuttle

exploration—the act of traveling through an unfamiliar area to learn more about it

external—outside

International Space Station—a place for astronauts from all over the world to work in outer space

launch pad—a platform from which a rocket is launched

mission—a task or a job

NASA—National Aeronautics and Space Administration; NASA is a U.S. government agency responsible for space travel and exploration.

orbit—a circular path around an object

orbiter—the part of a space shuttle designed to circle around a planet or moon

reusable—able to be used more than once

rocket boosters—parts that add additional thrust to aid in takeoff

satellites—objects in space that orbit a larger object

spacecraft—any vehicle used to travel in outer space

TO LEARN MORE

AT THE LIBRARY

Caper, William. *The Challenger Space Shuttle Explosion*. New York, N.Y.: Bearport Publishing Company, 2017.

Olivas, John D. *Endeavour's Long Journey: Celebrating 19 Years of Space Exploration*. Manhattan Beach, Calif.: East West Discovery Press, 2013.

West, David. *Spacecraft*. Mankato, Minn.: Smart Apple Media, 2017.

ON THE WEB

Learning more about space shuttles is as easy as 1, 2, 3.

1. Go to www.factsurfer.com.

2. Enter "space shuttles" into the search box.

3. Click the "Surf" button and you will see a list of related web sites.

With factsurfer.com, finding more information is just a click away.

INDEX